MY TURN BIBLE STORIES ABOUT OPPOSITES

Sarah Fletcher

Illustrated by Steve Edwards

CPH
SAINT LOUIS

1   2   3   4   5   6   7   8   9   10   08   07   06   05   04   03   02   01   00   99

This book belongs to

....

Birds fly UP in the sky.

So do bugs and bats. God made them that way.

Flowers
grow
DOWN
on the
ground.

God made them
that way. God
made everything
in the whole
world. God did a
good job.

Daniel's prayer was SOFT.

But his enemies
saw him pray.
They had Daniel
thrown into a pit
of lions.

6

The lions' roars were LOUD.

But God sent an angel to shut the mouths of the lions. God kept Daniel safe.

Jonah was OVER the water.

He was in a boat. Then God sent a storm. The sailors threw Jonah out of the boat.

Jonah was UNDER the water.

A fish swallowed Jonah. Jonah prayed to God. The fish spit him out. He was safe.

The sky
was DARK
when Jesus
was born.

Jesus, God's Son,
was born in a
stable with
animals all
around.

The sky was LIGHT when the angels sang.

An angel told the shepherds about baby Jesus. Then all the angels sang, "Glory to God!"

Peter's nets were EMPTY.

He had fished
all night and
caught nothing.
Jesus told Peter
to try again.

Then Peter's nets were FULL of fish.

But Peter left the fish behind. He wanted to follow Jesus.

Ten men were SICK.

They had a skin disease. It could kill them. Then they met Jesus.

Jesus made the ten men WELL.

But only one said, "Thank You." What do you think about that?

One little sheep was LOST.

·····················

The shepherd left 99 sheep behind. He looked for the lost one.

The little sheep was FOUND.

The shepherd was very happy. Jesus said God loves us and cares for us like a shepherd.

One son
was NEAR
his father.

He worked hard
at home.

One son went FAR away.

He made some wrong choices. But the father loved them both. God loves all of us too.

Zaccheus
was a
SHORT
man.
....
He wanted to
see Jesus.

The other people were TALL.

So Zacchaeus climbed a tree, and he saw Jesus. Jesus even became his friend.

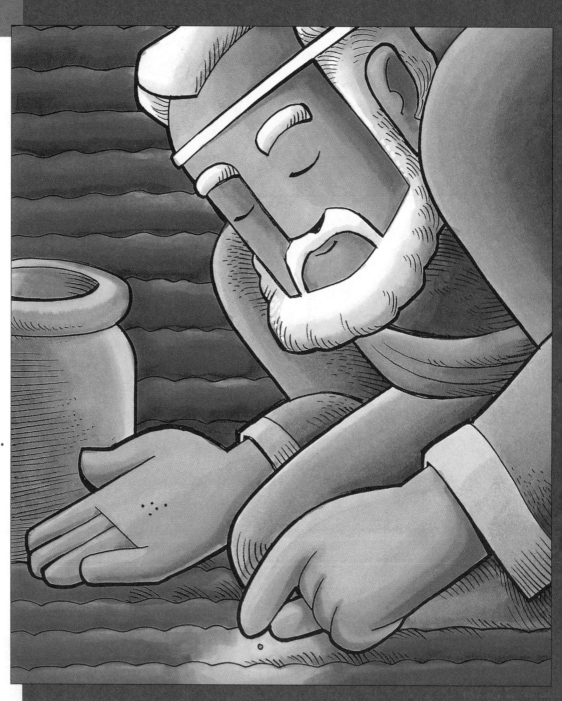

A mustard
seed is
very
LITTLE.

But when you
plant that seed,
something
wonderful
happens.

It grows into a BIG bush.

The birds can sit on its branches. The love of Jesus is big and wonderful too.

Martha was a BUSY woman.

She rushed here. She rushed there. She wanted everything to be perfect.

Mary sat very STILL.

She listened to everything Jesus said. Jesus said she did the right thing.

A little girl was DEAD.

But her father brought Jesus to their house.

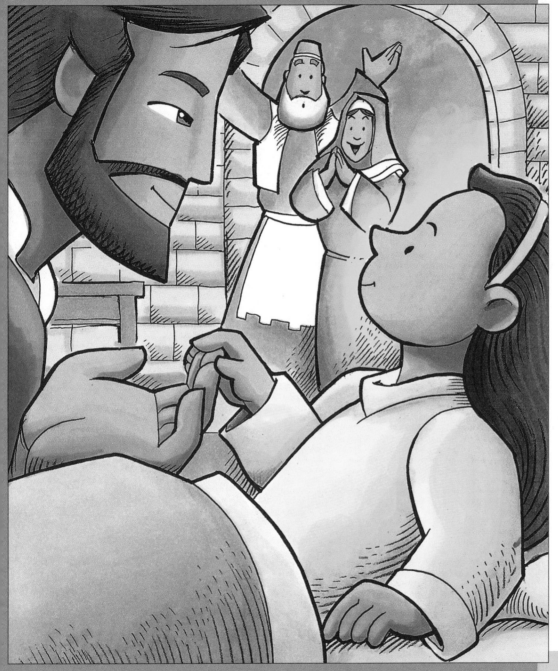

Jesus made the little girl ALIVE.

Everyone was glad. Jesus said, "Give her something to eat."

His friends were SAD when Jesus died.

....

He died on a cross. That was God's plan.

But they were HAPPY when God made Jesus alive.

· ·

That was God's plan too. And because of Jesus, we can be God's children— forever!

UP and
DOWN.
SOFT and
LOUD.

The world is full
of opposites.

BIG and LITTLE. SAD and HAPPY.

But God is God of all of them—even YOU and ME.

Dear Parent/Teacher:

This little book is packed with lots of learning activities for your children. First read the book to them all the way through. Let them study each picture as you talk about the opposites shown.

Then let them read the book to you, using only the top line on each page. Next you can take turns, the children reading the top lines and you reading the bottom lines. It won't be long before they can read the whole book alone!

Of course, the most important lesson in the book is that of God's unchanging love for the children, even in a world of opposites. Reinforce that lesson whenever you can.

 *The Editor*